Book Title:

# Top 10 Most Commonly Asked Farrier Questions: A guide for the horse owner.

# A "Farrier-Friendly"™ publication

---

## Published by:

## FARRIER-FRIENDLY™ SERVICES

Athens,  OH  45701

Website:  www.farrierfriendly.com
Email:   farrierfriendly@hotmail.com

Book Art work by: Julie Woodburn

# Table of Contents:

---

# Preface :

---

Whether you're a trainer, owner, or just a horse enthusiast, there will come a time when you will either be confronted with asking or answering certain hoof related questions. Though it is not realistic for anyone to *always* have the right answer on the tip of their tongue, it is reasonable to expect an equine professional or a responsible horse owner to at least have sufficient knowledge of how to access reliable sources of information.

With that in mind, as a professional working farrier, I've taken the previous 25 years of commonly asked farrier related questions and compiled a short list of the 10 most popular.

Since I have been given a great opportunity to practice the art of horseshoeing and horsemanship, I've learned many things about my craft. One of the most valuable to me is the notion that sometimes the best answers are often a result of learning how to ask the best questions. As a former instructor of farrier science, I still find this method to be extremely helpful and find myself often raising more questions before coming to any conclusive answers.

It is my intent that this guide will not only serve to answer some of those most commonly asked farrier questions, but also raise some new ones.  It is my hope that this "*Farrier-Friendly*"™  guide will enlighten you to new ideas or, at the very least, prevent you from being in the dark over those older ones.

Thank you for your interest in "*Farrier-Friendly*"™  and good luck as you continue your journey of learning with your horse.

Your friend in horses,

Bryan Farcus  MA,CJF-BWFA

# What are *your* TOP 10
## Farrier Questions ?

------------------------------------------------

#10 -

# 9 -

# 8 -

# 7 -

# 6 -

# 5 -

# 4 -

# 3 -

# 2 -

# 1 -

# Those Questions of Curiosity...

## THE UNANSWERED

An anonymous author once wrote:

"Everything that is either timeless or priceless comes to us in the form of art. Those things which are based on mechanics alone must be updated periodically and for a price."

Each time I read this passage, I am reminded of the importance of recognizing our work as an expression of art; where upon, to express ones self requires that we get in touch with our artistic abilities. These abilities are comparable to muscles—only through exercise will they develop and become definite. A master craftsman or artist in any field can have some difficulty explaining how his or her work turned out so beautifully. Similarly, an expert horseshoer can perform his or her work on such a level that there seems to be an indescribable beauty about it. On a fairly regular basis, I am approached by many different people and I receive a variety of questions.

The most difficult to explain are those that involve the "feel-of -

the- skill".  In all honesty,  the clearest

understanding of any art involves going   beyond

what any words could ever reveal.

## And THE EASILY ANSWERED

Fortunately, there are a few questions that are

simple and general enough to answer.  In top ten

order, they are as follows:

*#10-How can a person become a farrier?*

There are two ways to obtain the horseshoeing and

horsemanship skills that are necessary in order to

become a professional farrier.  One, is through a

Farrier Studies program at an accredited school and

the other is through a private apprenticeship program

offered by many older, more experienced farriers.

Personally, I recommend a combination of  both.  In

most cases, expect at least two years of basic

training.  Also, worth mentioning is the idea of

continuing education. This can be achieved through clinics, seminars, "ride-alongs" with more experienced farriers, or just simply taking some time to research new ideas.

## #9-*Is there a high risk of back injury?*

To honestly answer this question, I must start by saying that horseshoeing is a physical activity and just like any hands-on activity there is a chance of injury. However, there are two measures a farrier can take to lessen this risk. The first is to prepare for the activity by stretching and exercising. Many farriers do a daily routine of stretching the lower back muscles before doing their work; very similar to that of a baseball catcher before the start of each game. The second involves preparing the horse. Most often the majority of injuries result from failed attempts to shoe untrained horses. Forceful pressure or restraints put upon a horse will always increase the level of a horse's "trapped fear" and, in turn, that increases the farrier's odds of getting seriously injured. Instead, I recommend that we rely on a "lasting" training technique, in order to gain the horse's trust before attempting any horseshoeing.

## #8-Does a farrier get kicked often?

Any experienced farrier knows all too well about this. I think I'm not alone in saying that on an on-going, almost subconscious level the fear of getting kicked exists and the amount of risk a farrier assumes is based on his or her personal experiences. More definitively, I can say that by nature a horse will kick for one of two reasons: a) the threat of an attack , or b) becoming trapped. In my opinion, to lessen the risk of a kick and at the same time gain a more "lasting" control of the horse, the farrier should prescribe to the horse owner a logical horsemanship training technique. There are several <u>Basic Body Language Systems</u> (BBLS's) currently being used and promoted by successful trainers.

# #7-*Can you make a living as a farrier?*

According to recent survey published in the American Farrier's Journal, the annual income for a farrier can easily reach "six figures". This, of course, varies according to an individual's experience and demand factors.

# #6-*How much does it normally cost to have a horse shod?*

Depending on the extent of the work, which is based on the health of the horse's feet, the price (after calculating trip fees and recommended hoof care products) may often end up in the $100 range.

# #5-*How often do horses need farrier work?*

This will depend on the overall condition of the horse, the climate he lives in, and what his job is. On an average most farriers will recommend a visit every 6 to 8 weeks.

## #4-*Are there different shoes for different horses?*

Yes; Modern day horseshoeing requires that the farrier choose the shoes that will best support and protect the horse and at the same time allow him to perform. A qualified farrier will examine the conformation and movement patterns of a horse, in order to select the shoes that are most beneficial.

## #3-*Why do some horses need special shoes?*

In this situation, you may hear some farriers referring to the concept of "corrective" shoeing. Perhaps it is more easily explained if you consider this simple thought: "A horse is shod correctly if his shoes promote strong feet, strong legs and strong gaits (way of traveling)" . If for some reason a horse is weak in any one of these areas, special shoes could help. These are three of the most common situations: a) Weak, tender feet often bruise easily. Flat padded shoes can prevent such occurrences.

b) Weak limbs, resulting at birth or due to an injury can be supported by various combinations of bar shoes and/or Degree (wedged) pads.

And c), Occasionally, horses have trouble moving freely and this weakness in gaits could cause the horse to experience a hitting (interfering) of his limbs. Various toe or heel adjustments of the horse's shoe can improve the support, timing and direction of his footfall patterns.

## #2-*If the horses in the wild can survive without farrier work, why can't the others?*

The truly "wild horses" as we know them are a thing of the past. In modern times, horses are products of human influence. Being as it may, horses are now managed and even bred selectively to meet human standards. Unfortunately, these standards are not always in the horse's best interests. And, as a result, over the centuries weaker traits have become more dominant.  Remember, that in the actual wild only the strongest of stallions and mares successfully bred.  This was the natural order of selection, which in most cases produced stronger, healthier feet.

*And the #1 question, most often asked is...*

*Does nailing-on a shoe hurt the horse?*

If done properly, the horse does not experience any pain.  The keratinization process (division of dead cells) that occurs within the horse's hooves is the same as that of our finger and toe nail growth.  Within reason, you can cut through or reshape the nail.  Each time a farrier works on a horse's foot, he or she learns the quality or "vertical depth tolerance" differences that exist from one horse to another.  A competent farrier will spend hours practicing the mechanics of accurate nailing techniques.  These hours of practice can be compared to the countless number of bullets a marksman will fire at a target in an effort to become a sharp shooter. The ability to develop a strategic approach toward nail placement, along with the ability to analyze the health of each foot, is the key to keeping the shoeing process "horse-friendly".

## Glossary of Terms:

---

*Axis BB (Broken-Back):* hoof to pastern digit axis line that is visualized to represent a long toe/low heel hoof conformation.

*Axis BF (Broken-Forward):* hoof to pastern digit axis line that is visualized to represent a short toe/high heel hoof conformation.

*Bars:* viewed from the bottom of the hoof, minor protrusions present on both sides of the frog, a connective tissue that ties the buttress of the heel to the sole, acts to reinforce the heels.

*Bar shoe:* general term used to indicate any shoe that is closed or connected at the ends to maximize weight bearing surface, often used to stabilize a weak hoof or support a weakness in a limb.

*BBLS:* (Basic Body Language System) a term used to identify any system of communicating with the horse through herd instincts, based on predetermined gestures, signals, or cues that are horse logical.

# Glossary of Terms [continued] :

---

**Bulb:** located at the back of a hoof connecting the frog and the coronary band, often referred to as the frog band.

**Buttress of Heel:** the part of the hoof wall that runs to the open end of the foot, often referred to as the point or butt of the heel.

**Conformation:** an overall view of the horse's entire body, comparing the horse's body structure for symmetry and/or functional alignment.

**Commissures:** the grooves that are present on either side of the frog, sometimes referenced as the paracuneal sulci.

**Corrective shoeing:** an approach to shoeing with a major emphasis on changing the horse's stance and/or way of going.

**Coronary Band:** a band of soft tissue that surrounds the top of each hoof nearest the hairline.

## Glossary of Terms [continued]:

---

***Club footed:*** a hoof that grows excessively high in the heel as compared to the toe length, there are various degrees of severity, generally considered "clubby" if the horse's hoof- to-pastern is broken-forward, due to a flexor tendon contracture that is extreme enough to distend the coffin joint. This condition may be due to an injury, but most commonly inherited.

***Deep Digital Cushion:*** also know as the plantar cushion, a fibro-fatty tissue underlying the frog that functions as a shock absorber.

***Degree Pad:*** wedged shaped pads that are placed between the hoof and the shoe that will raise the hoof and lift the rear surface of a limb

***.Deviation:*** a departure from a predetermined ideal, a term often used in horse conformation analysis to describe crookedness in a limb.

# Glossary of Terms [continued] :

---

***Dynamic Hoof Balance:*** evaluation of hoof balance as it pertains to the horse in motion, considering how the hoof will land and load.

***Frog:*** a triangular shaped, elastic pad-like tissue that is located at the bottom of the foot that acts to absorb concussion and aid in traction

***Gait:*** a pattern of movement or the way in which the horse travels, certain gaits are natural to all horses but some can be artificial.

***Hoof Anatomy:*** the study of the structure/parts of a hoof.

***Hoof Physiology:*** the study of the function of a hoof

***.Interfering:*** a term used to describe the hitting together of a horse's foot to an opposing limb in a manner that restricts the horse's ability to move forward in a comfortable manner.

# Glossary of Terms [continued]:

---

***Keratination:*** a process whereby the division of horn producing cells accumulate to produce outer layers of hoof wall to protect sensitive tissue,similar to our nail.

***LLD (Limb Length Disparity):*** a condition where the horse suffers from a structural difference of his limbs as a working pair, often a curvature of the spine and/or a clubbed footed conformation is present.

***Low-Underrun Heels:*** When viewed from the side, the heels of the horse are collapsed and low to the ground, the slope or angle of the heel is much lower than that of the toe.

***Phalanx -1$^{st}$ :*** the first bone in the lower limb directly below the fetlock, also known as the long pastern.

***Phalanx -2$^{nd}$:*** the second bone in the lower limb directly below the fetlock, also known as the short pastern.

# Glossary of Terms [continued] :

---

*Quarter:* when viewed from the bottom of the hoof, the region of hoof wall that is between the toe and heel.

*Sensitive Laminae:* an interlocking, velcro-like tissue within a hoof that is responsible for connecting the hoof wall to the coffin bone.

*Seat of corn:* viewed from the bottom of the hoof, a junction where the edge of the bar, sole and white-line come together, an area susceptible to attracting debris that can result in a sore spot (corn).

*Sole:* the flat, ground surface portion of the hoof, responsible for creating a natural pad that is designed to protect the coffin bone.

*Static Hoof Balance:* a view of hoof balance when the horse is at a stand still, using a geometric reference (X,Y,Z planes) for a three dimensional perspective.

*Supportive Shoeing:* fitting a shoe with enough length and width to protect and support the entire limb.

# Glossary of Terms [continued] :

*Therapeutic Shoeing:* an approach to shoeing that provides a level of comfort and also attempts to remedy a hoof disease.

*Vertical Depth Tolerance:* a general reference to the amount of exfoliated sole that is able to be safely trimmed without causing the horse to be tender.

*White line:* usually yellowish or brown, it is the connective tissue (terminal ends of the sensitive laminea) that bonds the hoof wall to the sole, aids in nail placement.

# Helpful Tables & Graphics:

This page is reprinted with permission from the Author
 of **HORSE FOOT CARE** By Dr. Doug Butler

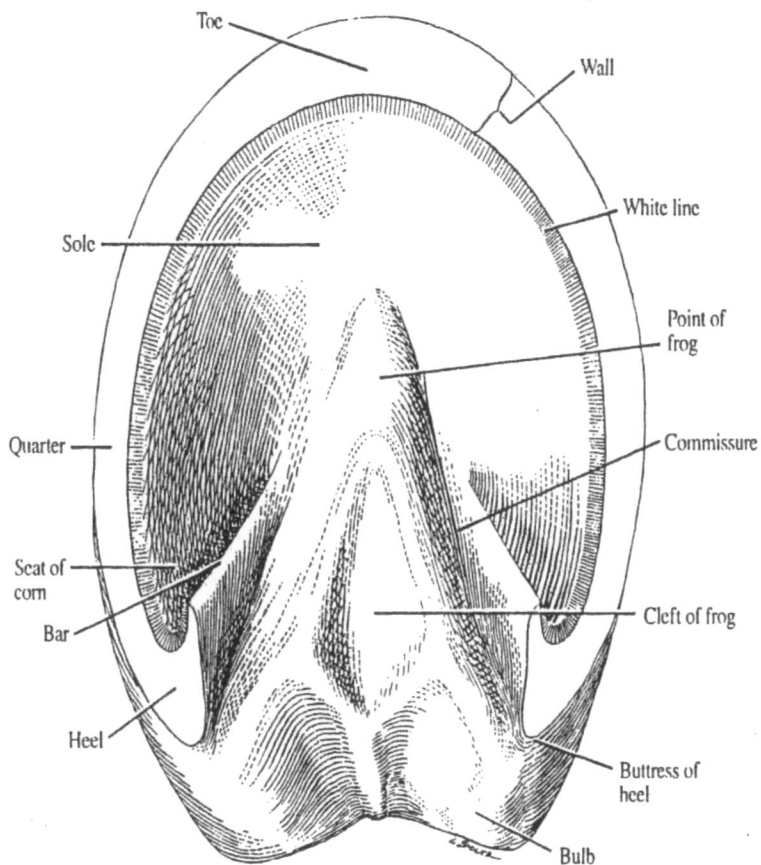

Toe

Wall

White line

Sole

Point of frog

Quarter

Commissure

Seat of corn

Cleft of frog

Bar

Heel

Buttress of heel

Bulb

*The parts of the hoof*

X

Y

Z

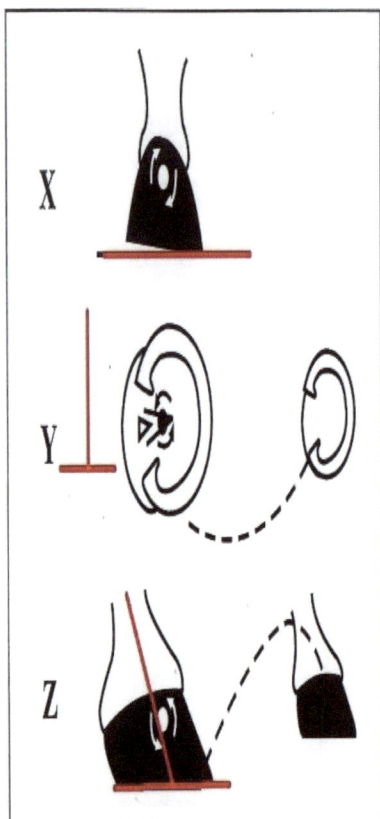

Visualing the 3 dimensions of balance as applied to Dynamic or Functional balance.

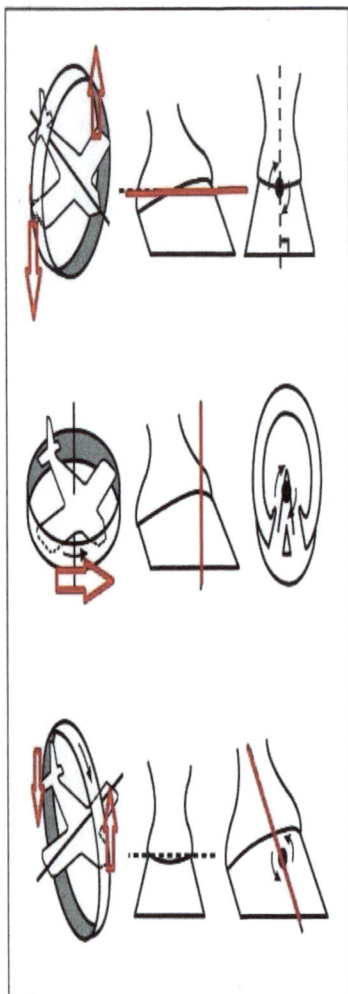

| A POSITIVE<br>*"A Healthy Hoof"* | ITS OPPOSITE<br>*"An Unhealthy Hoof"* |
|---|---|
| Hard/shiny exterior hoof wall. | Soft/cracked, dull exterior wall. |
| Symmetrically shaped hoof wall. | Asymmetrically shaped hoof wall. |
| Soft/flexible hair line tissues. | Hard/"crusty" hair line tissues. |
| Soft/flexible frog tissues. | Hard or diseased frog tissues. |
| Parallel growth pattern of toe and heel lengths. | Reversed growth pattern of toe and heel lengths. |
| Normal cupping of the sole.<br>(bottom surface of hoof is arched allowing for edge of hoof wall to contact ground first) | Extremely flat or "dropped" sole.<br>(bottom surface of hoof is contacting the ground before edge of hoof wall) |
| Hoof wall thickness approx. 2 x greater than "white line" thickness. | Hoof wall thickness less than the "white line" thickness<br>(white line distortion) |
| "White line" region and sole surface adjoin without deep cracks present. | Deep cracks existing between the "white line" region and the sole surface. |

©2001, Bryan Farcus

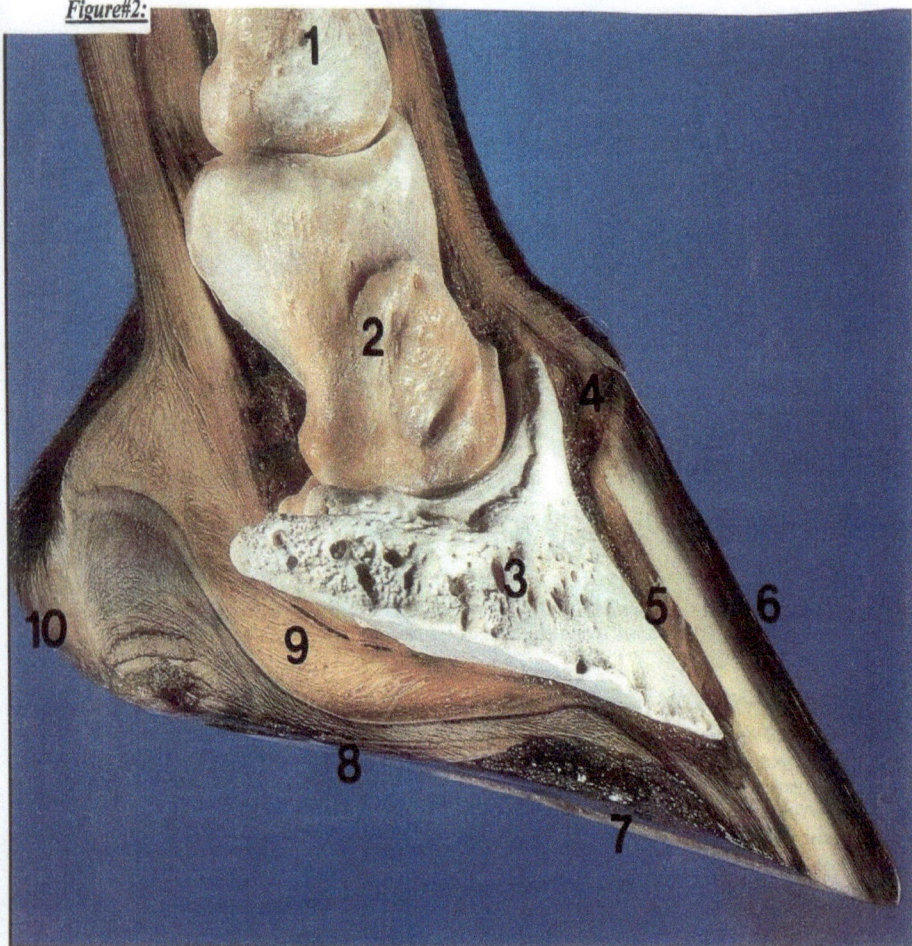

LATERAL OBLIQUE VIEW OF EQUINE DIGIT. Soft tissue is removed from one side of the phalanges.
Used by permission, courtesy of : The American Farriers Journal. ©1999 Lessiter Publications, Inc.

1. First Phalanx (long pastern).
2. Second Phalanx (short pastern).
3. Third Phalanx (coffin bone).
4. Coronary Band.
5. Sensitive Laminae.
6. Hoof wall (toe region).
7. Sole.
8. Frog.
9. Deep Digital Cushion.
10. Bulb of foot.

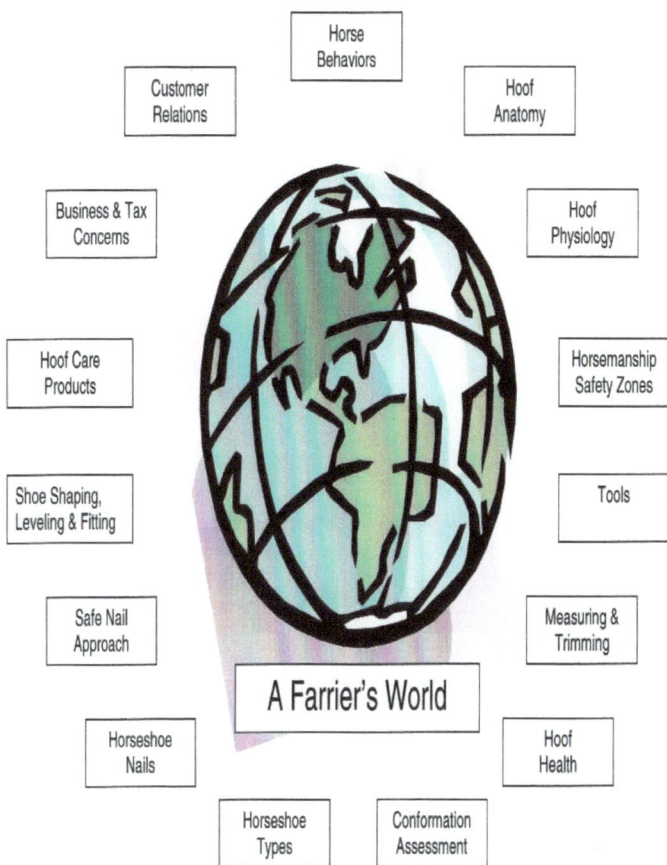

Horse Behaviors

Customer Relations

Hoof Anatomy

Business & Tax Concerns

Hoof Physiology

Hoof Care Products

Horsemanship Safety Zones

Shoe Shaping, Leveling & Fitting

Tools

Safe Nail Approach

Measuring & Trimming

A Farrier's World

Horseshoe Nails

Hoof Health

Horseshoe Types

Conformation Assessment

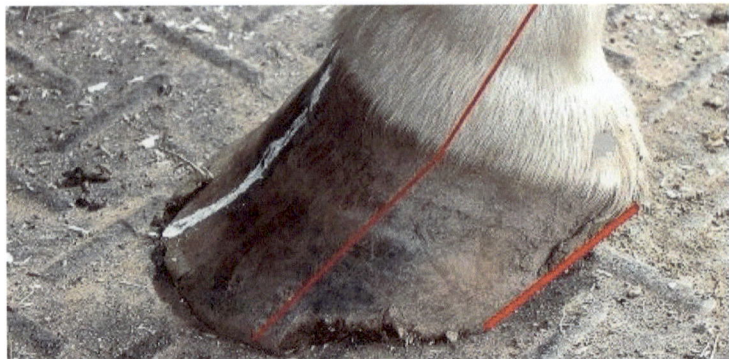

**Broken-Back Axis**

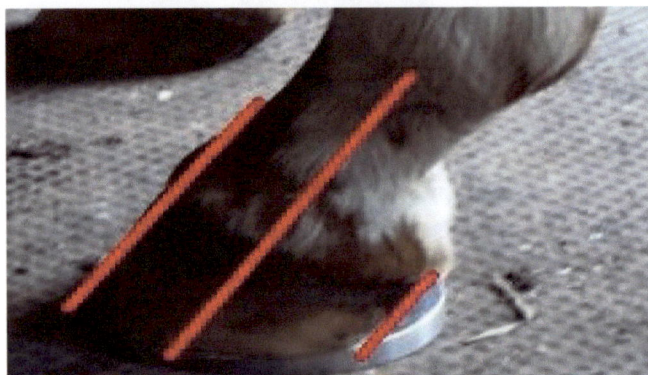

**Balanced**

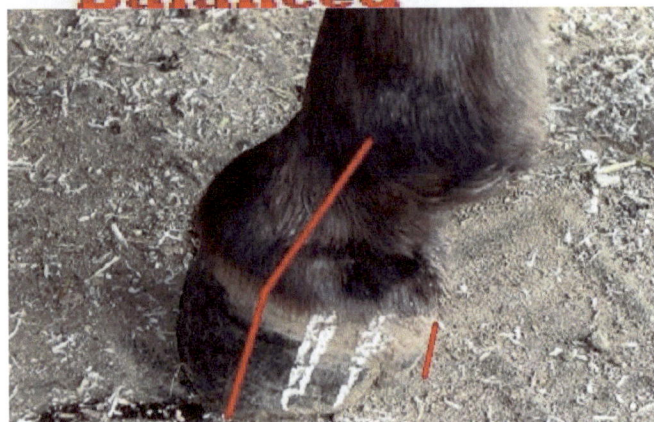

**Broken-Forward Axis**

Photos by: Bryan Farcus CJF

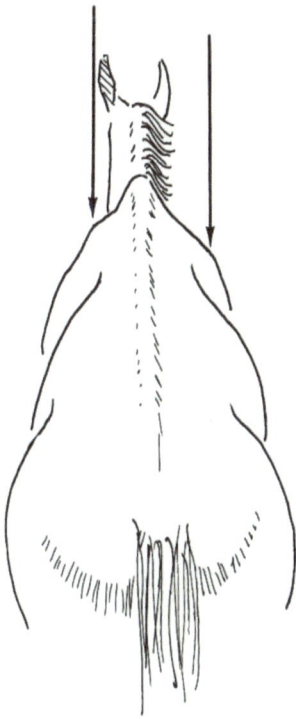

Diagram courtesy of King Lamadora

Photo courtesy of Kirk Underschultz CJF

Top-line imbalances can result due to a variety of conformational issues.   Of the most common are: *Club footedness, Low-underrun heels, Curvature of the spine, Dropped shoulder/or hip, Congenital bone length differences within limbs.*  Some are functional deviations while others are not.

## Limb Length Disparity (*LLD*)

# Resources & Recommending Reading :

## RESOURCES...

American Farrier's Journal , Lessiter Publications

PBM : A Diary of Lameness, Anthony Gonzales

Shoeing In Your Right Mind , Dr. Doug Butler

Six Figure Shoeing , Dr. Doug Butler

The Principles of Horseshoeing (P3),Doug &Jacob Butler

The Lame Horse , James Rooney DVM

## WEBSITES...

www.butlerprofessionalfarrierschool.com
www.myhorsematters.com
www.horseshoes.com

## ASSOCATIONS...

AAPF, American Association of Professional Farriers, www.professionalfarriers.com
AFA, American Farrier's Association, www.americanfarriers.org
BWFA, Brotherhood of Working Farriers, www.bwfa.net

# About The Author :

# *Bryan S. Farcus* MA, CJF-BWFA ~

For the past 25 years, Bryan has been combining the skills of horseshoeing, teaching, and riding. He is a Certified Journeyman Farrier through the Brotherhood of Working Farriers Association (BWFA) and also holds a certification in Equine Massage Therapy. Bryan's other accomplishments include both a Master of Arts degree with a specialization in equine education and a Bachelor of Science degree in the area of business.

For more than ten years, Bryan was the director/ instructor of a Farrier Studies program at an international equestrian college and a guest instructor for others, as well. These days, he continues his teaching by offering various "horsemanship for horseshoeing" programs. Upon invitation, Bryan presents demonstrations and group discussions on basic hoof care and horsemanship, in order to promote the advancement of equine education. Bryan is also the creator of a select line of *"Farrier-Friendly™"* products and currently authors a series of *"Farrier-Friendly™"* articles that appear in horse magazines throughout the US. Bryan currently works with horses and their owners in Ohio and West Virginia. You can visit him at: www.farrierfriendly.com or e-mail: farrierfriendly@hotmail.com

www.ingramcontent.com/pod-product-compliance
Lightning Source LLC
Chambersburg PA
CBHW041756050426
42443CB00023B/17